United States Department of Agriculture

Forest Service

Gen. Tech. Report WO-82a

September 2009

Forest Soil Disturbance Monitoring Protocol

Volume I: Rapid Assessment

By Deborah S. Page-Dumroese,
Ann M. Abbott, and Thomas M. Rice

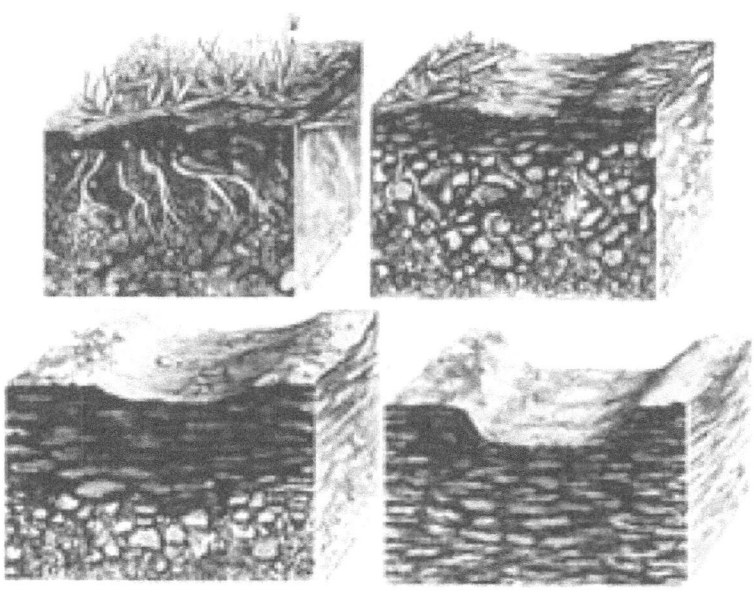

Schematics from Napper et al. (N.d.)

Disclaimer

CONTENTS

Acknowledgments

The monitoring approach and methods in volume I and volume II are the result of extensive collaboration between the Forest Service, U.S. Department of Agriculture National Forest System and Research and Development. The Forest Service Rocky Mountain Research Station in cooperation with the Northern Region led the effort. Although the development of this protocol has been guided by suggestions from a large number of regional soil program leaders, forest soil scientists, research soil scientists, university professors, and British Columbia Ministry of Forests and Range soil scientists, we particularly want to acknowledge the input and guidance from Sharon DeHart[1], Sue Farley[2], and Randy Davis[3]. Countless reviewers, workshop participants, students, and technicians have tested this protocol and offered input on how to make it more user friendly. Their input has been extraordinarily beneficial.

General Summary

This document—Volume I: Rapid Assessment—outlines a framework for monitoring soil disturbances from forest management preactivity and postactivity. Volume II: Supplementary Methods, Statistics, and Data Collection defines key terms, explains the development of a statistically sound data collection method, and describes how data should be stored. Volume III: Scientific Background for Soil Monitoring on National Forests and Rangelands includes the proceedings from a workshop held to define the state of the science. This volume outlines the step-by-step field protocols to get a rapid assessment of the disturbance characteristics before and after land management.

---

[1] Former Soil Program Leader, Northern Region, Missoula, MT.
[2] Forest Soil Scientist, Helena National Forest, Helena, MT.
[3] National Soil Program Leader, Washington Office, Washington, DC.

Introduction

This volume of the Forest Soil Disturbance Monitoring Protocol (FSDMP) describes how to monitor forest sites before and after ground disturbing management activities for physical attributes that could influence site resilience and long-term sustainability. The attributes describe surface conditions that affect **site sustainability** and **hydrologic function.** Monitoring the attributes of surface cover, ruts, compaction, and platy structure can also be used to generate best management practices that help maintain **site productivity.**

Key Monitoring Points

The Forest Soil Disturbance Monitoring Protocol describes surface conditions that affect—

- Site sustainability.
- Hydrologic function.
- Site productivity.

This protocol is intended to be used by field soil scientists and watershed specialists when evaluating physical soil disturbance in a forested setting. This *rapid assessment tool* can also be useful, however, for timber sale administrators, logging contractors, hydrologists, and the general public to help them understand how to monitor soil disturbance using standardized visual disturbance classes. Monitoring soil disturbance preactivity and postactivity enables the Forest Service to assess the success of management activities in meeting legal, regulatory, and policy objectives. By using a consistent monitoring approach, forests in every Forest Service region can build soil resource programs to meet their specific requirements in accord with their soil quality standards and guidelines. Table 1 provides common definitions of frequently used soil descriptors.

Table 1.—*Visual indicators and their definitions.*

Forest floor impacted	Forest floor material includes all organic horizons above the mineral soil surface.
Topsoil displacement	The surface mineral soil primarily includes the A horizons, but if the A horizon is shallow or undeveloped, it may include other horizons. This disturbance is usually due to machinery but does not include "rutting" described below.
Rutting	Ruts vary in depth but are primarily the result of equipment movement. Ruts are defined as machine-generated soil displacement or compression. Often soil puddling is also present within the rut.
Burning (light, moderate, severe) severity	Burn severity includes only effects on the forest floor and mineral soil, not on above-ground vegetation.
Compaction	Compaction by equipment results in either a compression of the soil profile or increased resistance to penetration.
Platy structure/ massive/puddled	Flat-lying or tabular structure in the mineral soil. "Massive" indicates no structural units are present and soil material is a coherent mass. Puddled soil is often found after wet weather harvest operations. Soil pores are usually smeared and prevent water infiltration.

Objective

The FSDMP defines indicators that can be measured consistently, efficiently, and economically. It is intended for use in any forested activity area to set the stage to address and report project effects. The FSDMP provides estimates of soil disturbance and confidence intervals around the monitoring results. The estimates are based on sample sizes calculated from the onsite variability estimated from the first 30 monitoring points in the sample and a predetermined confidence level. The following chart shows the rapid assessment steps.

Rapid Assessment Steps

Steps
Define the monitoring objective (preactivity, postactivity, short-term monitoring, long-term monitoring, etc.).
Gather the necessary background information—soil survey, maps, photos, etc.—and determine if the site should be stratified. Enter site description data on FSDMPSoLo worksheet #1 (SoLo Info).
Decide on confidence level (FSDMP worksheet #3 – Data Entry), transect design, and indicators needed (FSDMP worksheet #2 – Variable Selection).
Describe site management, slope, soil texture, soil depth, aspect, landform or topography, and elevation (FSDMP worksheet #1 – Data Entry).
Begin monitoring (FSDMP worksheet #3 – Data Entry).
Summarize results (FSDMP worksheet #4 - Results).

Transect Options

Option 1. Randomly Oriented Transects

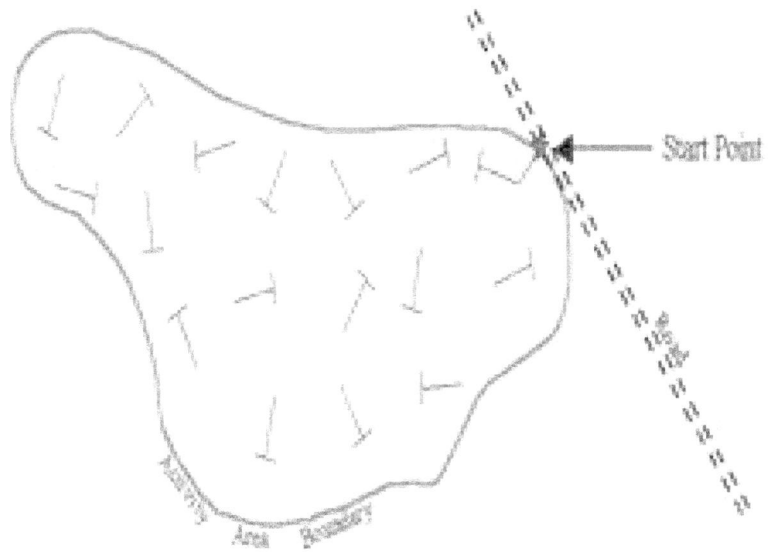

In this option transects are laid out randomly on a site map before going to the field. Monitoring points can be collected along these randomly established transects to collect the minimum number of points needed. At each intersection, a 30 m (~100 ft) transect is established. The attributes are then noted at monitoring points located along each transect.

Option 2. Systematic Grid Points

In this option the protocol calls for establishing a systematic grid of monitoring points arrayed on a map or aerial photograph of the activity area to be monitored. The entire grid is randomly located and oriented, and the distance between monitoring points is constructed to provide a sample size that meets precision requirements or cost limitations specified in the objectives for monitoring. Each grid intersection locates a monitoring point that radiates in a random chosen direction and distance from the grid point (Howes 2006).

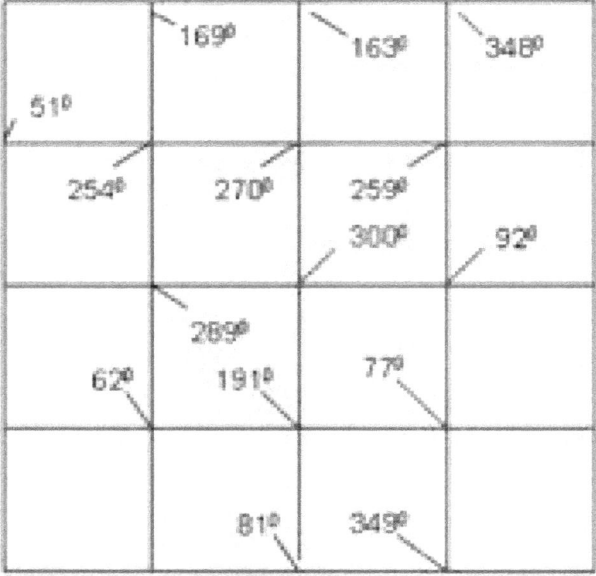

Option 3. A Random Transect

In this option the protocol calls for randomly locating a start point and traversing a transect that covers the entire unit so that the first 30 monitoring points (the minimum required) are spaced to provide an adequate assessment of the site. The entire transect is randomly located and oriented, and the distance between monitoring points is constructed to provide a sample size that meets precision requirements or cost limitations specified in the objectives for monitoring. Turning points are usually located within the activity area so that the last monitoring point before a turn is not within an area of influence of the surrounding stand (usually the height of the tallest trees). Additional transects at random directions are often needed to reach the appropriate sample size. If the transect begins to follow a skid road, either offset from the skid road or start a new random transect. Record offset or new direction.

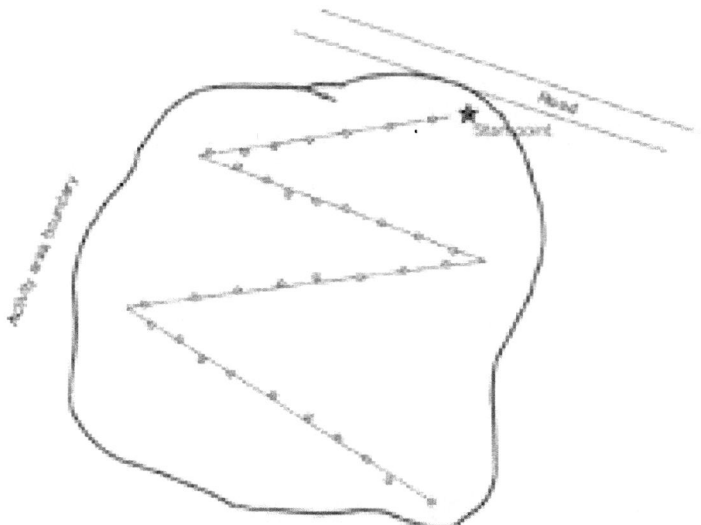

How Many Monitoring Points Do I Need?

The *minimum* number of monitoring points is 30. This minimum number is required to get site-specific variability for statistically valid sample size, and these 30 points should be conducted as a rapid assessment using the soil indicators selected. Only when the variability within the site is very small will the minimum of

30 be the final number of monitoring points. As the variability in disturbance within the site increases, so does the sample size required to achieve a confidence interval using a predetermined confidence level and interval width. If fewer than 30 monitoring points are taken, the sample sizes and confidence intervals calculated in the spreadsheet may be incorrect. The consequence of using more than 30 samples, but fewer than the number that the spreadsheet recommends, is that the confidence interval will be wider than the predetermined width, as indicated by the "Lower Bound" and "Upper Bound" values on the spreadsheet. Volume II addresses details of the formulas used for calculating sample size, the available confidence levels, and alternatives for varying sampling intensity.

We strongly recommend entering the data into the electronic spreadsheet rather than using the paper data collection form, because calculation of the intervals by hand is tedious and error prone. Summary levels of disturbance classes are also provided in the electronic *Results* worksheet (see appendix C-4 in volume II). Because disturbance class is an ordinal variable (meaning that levels of this variable are ordered categories), confidence intervals are not calculated.

For details on how to stratify sample points within a project area or about stratifying the number of project areas to sample, see volume II.

What Is a Monitoring Point?

For the FSDMP, a monitoring point is defined as a 15-cm (6-in) diameter circular area around the end of your toe. The presence or absence of each disturbance indicator at the point is noted. The visual disturbance class of each sample point is determined using the most limiting visual indicator at the point (table 2). Areas outside the monitoring point can be used for determining the general context of the disturbance but should not be used to decide the class of the point. Using the surrounding areas to determine the disturbance class would bias the sample system, especially if applied differently to different visual attributes.

Table 2.—*Soil disturbance classes used in the Forest Soil Disturbance Monitoring Protocol. Soil disturbance classes increase in severity of impact from class 0 to class 3. (1 of 2)*

Soil disturbance class 0	Soil disturbance class 1
Soil surface: • No evidence of compaction; i.e., past equipment operation, ruts, skid trails. • No depressions or wheel tracks evident. • Forest floor layers present and intact. • No soil displacement evident. • No management-generated soil erosion. • Litter and duff layers not burned. No soil char. Water repellency may be present.	Soil surface: • Faint wheel tracks or slight depressions evident and are <5 cm deep. • Forest floor layers present and intact. • Surface soil has not been displaced and shows minimal mixing with subsoil. • Burning light: Depth of char <1 cm. **Accessory***: Litter charred or consumed. Duff largely intact. Water repellency is similar to preburn conditions. Soil compaction: • Compaction in the surface soil is slightly greater than observed under natural conditions. • Concentrated from 0 to 10 cm deep. Observations of soil physical conditions: • Change in soil structure from crumb or granular structure to massive or platy structure; restricted to the surface 0 to 10 cm. • Platy structure is noncontinuous. • Fine, medium, and large roots can penetrate or grow around the platy structure. No "J" rooting observed. • Erosion is slight.

Table 2.—*Soil disturbance classes used in the Forest Soil Disturbance Monitoring Protocol. Soil disturbance classes increase in severity of impact from class 0 to class 3. (2 of 2)*

Soil disturbance class 2	Soil disturbance class 3
Soil surface: • Wheel tracks or depressions are 5 to 10 cm deep. • *Accessory**: Forest floor layers partially intact or missing. • Surface soil partially intact and may be mixed with subsoil. • Burning moderate: Depth of char is 1 to 5 cm. *Accessory**: Duff deeply charred or consumed. Surface soil water repellency increased compared with the preburn condition. Soil compaction: • Increased compaction is present from 10 to 30 cm deep. Observation of soil physical condition: • Change in soil structure from crumb or granular structure to massive or platy structure; restricted to the surface, 10 to 30 cm. • Platy structure is generally continuous. • *Accessory*:* Large roots may penetrate the platy structure, but fine and medium roots may not. • Erosion is moderate.	Soil surface: • Wheel tracks and depressions highly evident with depth >10 cm. • *Accessory**: Forest floor layers missing. • Evidence of surface soil removal, gouging, and piling. • Most surface soil displaced. Surface soil may be mixed with subsoil. Subsoil partially or totally exposed. • Burning severe: Depth of char is >5 cm. *Accessory**: Duff and litter layer completely consumed. Surface soil is water repellent. Surface is reddish or orange in places. Soil compaction: • Increased compaction is deep in the soil profile (>30 cm deep). Observations of soil physical conditions: • Change in soil structure from granular structure to massive or platy structure extends beyond 30 cm deep. • Platy structure is continuous. • *Accessory**: Roots do not penetrate the platy structure. • Erosion is severe and has produced deep gullies or rills.

*Accessory items are those descriptors that may help identify individual severity classes.

Unique Monitoring Strategies

Volume II outlines the details of unique monitoring strategies. These strategies provide a standardized protocol for assessing large and small units; determining how many activity areas to monitor; and deciding how to count rocks, roots, downed wood, stumps, fallen trees, slash piles (containing tree tops, branches, brush, etc.) and so on that fall on a sample point. Volume II also standardizes descriptions of how to assess prescribed fire and wildfire areas and defines landings and temporary and permanent roads that fall within the scope of the FSDMP.

Soil Disturbance Classes

Table 2 shows a four-level soil disturbance classification system. Disturbance classes used in the FSDMP are defined primarily by morphological (visual) attributes, not quantitative measures. In this visual class system, an increased severity of soil surface disturbance indicates a change in the disturbance class. Some changes (such as compaction and rutting), however, are linked to an increase in that property at depth. Evidence of deep soil compaction (e.g., deep ruts) is often present but not always. A shovel or metal probe may be needed if deep soil compaction is questionable. Because the results of management activities on soil productivity vary by soil type (Fleming et al. 2006, Gomez et al. 2002, Page-Dumroese et al. 2000, Page-Dumroese et al. 2006, Powers et al. 1998), this document does not prescribe any disturbance class as detrimental soil disturbance. Each Forest Service administrative region should determine where and when a detrimental call should be made based on local knowledge, research, and experience. Often, the definition of detrimental disturbance is tied to existing soil quality standards and guidelines. After the determination of detrimental disturbance is defined and noted, then this FSDMP can be used to calculate the amount of detrimental disturbance (e.g., if 5 out of 100 sample points are considered in a detrimental condition, then 5 percent of the area has been detrimentally disturbed).

As the activity area is walked, each monitoring point is placed in one of the predefined classes. The monitoring point may represent soil indicators from more than one soil disturbance class, and the soil scientist or other observer must decide which disturbance class best describes the monitoring point.

Local, forest-level class descriptors can be added to table 2, but the core descriptors outlined in this volume cannot be removed. For classes to remain consistent among administrative units, core descriptors cannot be changed. If a core classification descriptor is found to be lacking applicability across many forests, the classification descriptor will undergo a regional and research review and the protocol will be updated if needed. (See volume II for information about change management.)

Safety

A sample job hazard analysis has been included in this volume as appendix A. Each national forest is encouraged to modify the job hazard analysis to suit local conditions and safety concerns.

What Data Should I Collect?

Data To Collect While in the Office

Before starting a field evaluation of soil disturbance on an activity area, study available existing information sources and record applicable information in the *SoLo Info* electronic worksheet (see appendix C-1 in volume II and additional details in appendix G in volume II). Having information on soil texture, landform, aspect, and so on will provide a context for the data and provide information for long-term monitoring (if needed). In general, the following steps should be followed before going into the field:

1. Consult the most current subsection map (McNab et al. 2007) and available landtype association maps for general site characteristics. The SoLo database may require some of this information, which can help stratify the area for sampling. It is important to note, however, that such broad-scale maps are not appropriate for the more detailed site information needed to assess soil quality.

2. Consult available soil surveys and terrestrial ecological unit inventories (TEUIs) for more detailed site information and for the description and morphology of the soils that occur in the project area. Soil surveys may have been done by the Forest Service or by the Natural Resources Conservation Service (NRCS) and may be referred to as soil resource inventories, TEUIs, or landtype inventories. This information can help establish soil reference conditions for the activity area. It is critical, however, to confirm the actual soil type after you are in the field.

3. Check previous field review and soil monitoring reports and use available data.

4. For postharvest assessments, consult the harvest plan and contract information to determine where existing skid trails, landings, or changes in harvest operations may have occurred.

Step-by-Step Field Survey Method

Before starting field work, ensure that the *SoLo Info* worksheet (see appendix C-1 in volume II) is as complete as possible, then determine the intensity of sampling (confidence level and interval width) with input from a line officer. As noted earlier, the area for the visual assessment is a 15-cm (6-in) diameter circular area around the monitoring point. Continuous variables such as ruts, skid trails, or landings can be measured (using a tape measure, laser measure, etc.) and the total area and areal extent of the disturbance can be calculated using the "ONSITE" feature of the database. If a survey of skid trails, landings, or ruts indicates excess (based on regional soil quality standards and guidelines) detrimental soil disturbance, then it is likely that further assessment is not necessary because the applicable soil quality standard has already been exceeded. If the large features do not exceed the maximum area for disturbance, however, the FSDMP assessment may be warranted. If no large features are in the activity area, a rapid assessment may be sufficient on some activity areas to confirm that the applicable soil quality standards have been met.

Choose the visual disturbance category by selecting the one best fitting the monitoring point. This protocol is to be used in cases in which activity areas are defined and discrete. For assessment of areas in a watershed context, without defined and discrete activity units, see this volume's section titled "Unique Monitoring Strategies."

Baseline (Preactivity) Assessment

Step 1. Prework—Determine why you are monitoring (goals) and if the FSDMP is the most efficient method for accomplishing those goals. As noted in the section titled "Data To Collect While in the Office," fill out as much of the electronic or paper form as possible using existing documentation and interviews with other team members (see also appendix G in volume II). Inspection of topographic maps and areal photography can reveal basic landform information, such as slope and drainage patterns that affect soil productivity or hydrologic function. Select the variables you want to use for monitoring the activity area (*Variable Selection* worksheet, appendix C-2 in volume II). Determine the size of the activity area. Determine which option for monitoring point layout will work best for your site (see appendix A in volume II). If choosing a random transect, select the length of transect needed and the distance between points. If choosing a grid point survey, select a random orientation for the grid points. If using an electronic portable data recorder, predetermine grid point locations and save them onto the recorder.

Step 2. Select the *Data Entry* worksheet (see appendix C-3 in volume II). If past ground-disturbing activities (e.g., stumps, skid trails, roads, differences in vegetation age or composition, or trash) are evident, continue to use the FSDMP for a quantitative estimate of the amount and extent of disturbance. Often, aerial photos and other maps can be used to determine the extent of effects. Field verification of compaction, displacement, or change in hydrologic state is necessary on sites with legacy effects. From preactivity assessments, determination of cumulative effects may be facilitated. Conversely, if records of previous management resulted in minimal soil disturbance and the activity area has similar soils, vegetation, aspect, and slope throughout the unit, then space a *minimum* of 30 monitoring points to cover the entire unit. When using the sample size calculator and appropriate confidence level, more points may be necessary. Take note of preactivity forest floor depth and composition, mineral soil horizon depth(s), and depth to bedrock (if applicable).

Step 3. Document a preactivity starting point using a Global Positioning System or other method of precise point location documentation. Using the sampling scheme selected from step 1, start sampling 5 m (~15 ft) inside the unit to avoid edge effects. If using a portable data recorder (see appendix F in volume II), upload a map of the site and add predetermined monitoring point locations before going into the field. Predetermining monitoring point locations can also be done with paper copies of available maps.

Step 4. After locating the starting point within the activity area, calculate the distance between points based on activity area size. To avoid bias, sample point distances must be predetermined and documented before starting. Points must be evenly spaced to cover the entire activity area. For instance, if the activity area is ~1,000 m (3,300 ft) long and you need to take 30 sample points, points should be at least 35 m (110 ft) apart along the random transect. If the transect (or point grid) does not adequately cover the range of variability, then take more transects (or grid points) to confirm the presence or absence of dispersed disturbance and the nature of the dispersed disturbance.

Step 5. Walk to the first point and assess the soil surface condition using the *Data Entry* worksheet (see appendix C-3 in volume II). On the data form, record a "1" if the indicator is present and a "0" if the indicator or statement is absent, ending with a general Soil Disturbance Class (using table 3). For assistance with visual class determinations, use the *Soil Disturbance Field Guide* Napper et al. N.d.). Continue collecting data at each monitoring point along the transect (grid). When you reach the edge of the activity area, select another transect direction (a predetermined grid point sampling scheme should be placed entirely within the activity area boundary) at an appropriate angle (toward the inside of the activity area) from the previous transect and continue data collection on the same spreadsheet. Note that, as you make observations at each monitoring point, the required sample size will likely change as the estimated variability changes.

Step 6. Continue the assessment until you reach the appropriate sample size. On the data form, record a "1" if the indicator is present and a "0" if the indicator or statement is absent, ending with a general soil disturbance class (table 2). *Take AT LEAST 30 monitoring points in the activity area that has disturbance.* Use aerial photos, ONSITE, or activity area maps to measure temporary roads and landings within or contiguous to the activity area, but take additional notes. Estimate disturbance on temporary roads or landings not in the activity area separately and manually add after completing this method.

Step 7. Use the comment field at the bottom of each column (or a field notebook) to document noteworthy existing disturbance. Use these comments to document unusual spatial features related to the disturbances or to record the type and severity of erosion features.

Step 8. In the last row of the *Data Entry* worksheet (see appendix C-3 in volume II) indicate if the soil disturbance is detrimental. This row of information is based on the professional judgment of a qualified soil scientist, literature, or other local studies.

Table 3.—*Examples of soil visual indicators and management activities. (1 of 3)*

Disturbance type	Severity class			
	0	1	2	3
Equipment impacts				
Past operation	None.	Dispersed.	Faint.	Obvious.
Wheel tracks or depressions	None.	Faint wheel tracks or slight depressions evident (<5 cm deep).	Wheel tracks or depressions are >5 cm deep.	Wheel tracks or depressions highly evident with a depth being >10 cm.
Equipment trails from more than two passes	None.	Faintly evident.	Evident, but not heavily trafficked.	Main trails that are heavily used.
Excavated and bladed trails[1]	None.	None.	None.	Present.

Disturbance type	Severity class			
	0	1	2	3
Penetration and resistance[2]	Natural conditions.	Resistance of surface soils may be slightly greater than observed under natural conditions. Increased resistance is concentrated in the surface (10 cm).	Increased resistance is present throughout the top 30 cm of soil.	Increased resistance is deep into the soil profile (>30 cm).
Soil physical condition	Natural conditions.	Change in soil structure from crumb or granular structure to massive or platy structure in the surface (10 cm).	Change in soil structure in the surface (30 cm). Platy (or massive) structure is generally continuous. On older sites, large roots may penetrate the platy structure, but fine and medium roots may not.	Change in soil structure extends beyond the top 30 cm. Platy (or massive) structure is continuous. On older sites, roots do not penetrate the platy structure.
Displacement				
Forest floor	None.	Forest floor layers present and intact.	Forest floor layers partially intact or missing.	Forest floor layers missing.

Table 3.—*Examples of soil visual indicators and management activities. (3 of 3)*

Disturbance type	Severity class			
	0	1	2	3
Mineral soil	None.	Soil surface has not been displaced and shows minimal mixing with subsoil.	Mineral topsoil partially intact and may be mixed with subsoil.	Evidence of topsoil removal, gouging, and piling. Soil displacement has removed most of the surface soil. Surface soil may be mixed with subsoil or subsoil may be partially or totally exposed.
Erosion	None.	Slight erosion evident (i.e., sheet erosion[3]).	Moderate amount of erosion evident (i.e., sheet and rill erosion[3]).	Substantial amount of erosion evident. Gullies, pedestals, and rills noticeable.
Burning	None.	Fire impacts are light. Forest floor is charred but intact. Gray ash becomes inconspicuous and surface appears lightly charred to black. Soil surface structure intact.	Fire impacts are moderate. Litter layer is consumed and humus layer is charred or consumed. Mineral soil not visibly altered, but soil organic matter (OM) has been partially charred.	Fire impacts are deep. The entire forest floor is consumed and top layer of mineral soil is visibly altered. Surface mineral structure and texture are altered. Mineral soil is black due to charred or deposited OM or is orange from burning.

[1] *Evaluate on main trails but not necessarily for wheel tracks or depressions.*

[2] *Soil resistance to penetration with a tile spade or probe is best done when the soil is not moist or wet.*

[3] *See USDA NRCS (1993).*

Postactivity Assessment

Step 1. Before starting work in an activity area, examine the soil in a nearby undisturbed unit for forest floor thickness, composition, mineral soil horizon depth(s), and depth to bedrock (if applicable). If baseline data have been collected (as in baseline assessment step 2), then this examination procedure may not be necessary. Examining an undisturbed area is essential, however, if one observer recorded the preactivity data and another observer is collecting the postactivity data. If an undisturbed site is not available, examine the undisturbed soil around stumps to become familiar with uncompacted soil conditions. Decide on the type of monitoring transect needed and locate a starting point using a method similar to that used for the preactivity assessment. It is not necessary to replicate transect locations from the previous assessment. The required sample size is likely to be different because of the increased variability of the site postactivity. It is better to complete two different assessments within the activity area.

Step 2. Using the procedure described for preactivity assessments, determine the soil surface disturbance. Record data points until you have taken enough monitoring points to reach the sample size calculated by the electronic spreadsheet or shown on the paper sample size table.

As in steps 7 and 8 (in the preactivity assessment), indicate the disturbance class for each point and indicate which points are considered detrimentally disturbed and would affect long-term site sustainability.

Filling Out the Field Form

The worksheet forms for the FSDMP provide for a core set of attributes that are important for linking soil disturbance to changes in site productivity. Although these forms represent a core data set, however, on some sites they may not be an expected attribute of the site. The soil indicators may also represent a more intense sampling scheme than is required for the monitoring objectives. By varying the sampling intensity and turning some attributes "off," you can still collect some of the soil indicators but be more efficient at data collection. The forms were designed so that a rapid assessment of soil disturbance would consistently look at a standard set of soil disturbance indicators; collecting this standard set of data is the reason why you must fill out each column completely before moving on to the next monitoring point. Do not modify the soil indicators on either the electronic or paper forms; the forms were designed to make data entry into the SoLo database quick and easy.

Site Descriptors and Soil Indicators

Each monitored activity area must have the required site descriptors included on the reports. These descriptors and their definitions are located in appendix G of volume II.

Detailed definitions about soil indicators used in the FSDMP appear in volume II. Table 3 illustrates the visually recognizable attributes of each indicator. When assessing soil indicators, each indicator can place the monitoring point into a different soil disturbance class. You must decide which feature is the overriding concern (based on soil texture, expected vegetative response, or site sensitivity) and to which soil disturbance class the monitoring point will be assigned.

Machine Traffic Disturbances

Use the ONSITE worksheet to calculate large features and determine the areal extent of skid trails, ruts, and landings. If the areal extent of these features is over the regional limit for detrimental disturbance, additional monitoring may or may not be needed.

Compaction

The *Data Entry* worksheet (see appendix C-3 in volume II) has three rows that list compaction (by depth). Determine the maximum extent of compaction and record a "1" (present) in the appropriate cell for that monitoring point. Record a "0" in each of the other two rows. If compaction occurs throughout the profile (not at one depth), then place a "1" in each cell for compaction. Visual indicators of change in compaction level are past operations (from aerial photos or databases), wheel tracks or depressions (ruts), equipment trails (e.g., from more than two passes), excavated or bladed trails, penetration resistance, and a change in structure.

Insert a metal rod or shovel into the ground to determine changes in the compaction level of a monitoring point. This surrogate for bulk density sampling can be effective if undisturbed soils are nearby to calibrate this "push" test. You must calibrate yourself to the physical resistance of each soil type. Although a change in compaction is often measured by pushing a rod or spade into the soil (or taking a bulk density core), the visual attributes listed previously (wheel tracks, equipment trails, etc.) may be all that is necessary to determine a change in surface disturbance.

Placing compaction into a soil disturbance class (disturbance class 1, 2, or 3) is based on depth of compaction change into the mineral soil. Because of this depth relationship, it is important to know the undisturbed condition (at depths) of the soil preactivity.

Rutting and/or Wheel Track Impressions

The *Data Entry* worksheet (see appendix C-3 in volume II) has three rows in which ruts are listed (by depth). Determine the maximum extent of the rut and record a "1" (present) in the cell for that monitoring point. Record a "0" in each of the other two rows. To measure the depth of the rut, you may need to determine where the approximate surface of the undisturbed soil is (or was). As mentioned previously, you can measure these physical features for area (length multiplied by the average width) and enter them into ONSITE to determine areal extent. Wheel tracks or ruts (impressions in the soil caused by heavy equipment) vary in depth and width. On sites that have a high compaction hazard (e.g., fine-textured soils, steep slopes), a shallow rut may cause degradation in site quality by altering the flow of water and gasses in the soil and/or increasing soil penetration resistance. On sites that have a low compaction hazard (e.g., coarse-textured soils), deeper ruts may not cause a detrimental change to water and gas flow but may represent displacement of fertile topsoil layers. Regardless of texture, however, wheel tracks and ruts can cause water to be routed off a site, making it unavailable for plant growth. Within a rut or wheel track could also be altered soil structure, increased soil density, puddling, compacted deposits of forest floor, fine slash, and woody debris (not readily excavated with a shovel). Placing ruts and wheel tracks into a soil disturbance category (disturbance class 1, 2, or 3) is based on their depth on the soil surface and their extension into the mineral soil profile.

Soil Structure

Record massive/platy/puddled soil on the *Data Entry* worksheet (see appendix C-3 in volume II). Determination of a change in structure is by depth and can sometimes be linked to the change in compaction level at the same depth. Determine the maximum extent of the change in structure and record a "1" (present) in the cell for that monitoring point. Record a "0" in each of the other two rows, unless these structural changes extend beyond one depth. In that case, record a 1 in each field.

Massive, platy, and puddled structures are indicators of a change in soil structure and a reduction in pore sizes that will change pore size distribution. Massive soil can be naturally occurring or can be caused by management activities. Massive structure means structural units are not present and the soil is a coherent mass. Platy structure can also be naturally occurring, but coarse-platy structure that has flat or tabular-like (dinner plate) units within the profile is usually caused by harvesting equipment. Puddled soils occur when equipment operates when the soil is too wet; soil is smeared along a wheel track or rut and causes water to pond on the surface. The change in soil physical conditions and their depth into the mineral soil profile will determine in which soil disturbance category (severity class) you will place it.

Surface Organic Matter

The *Data Entry* worksheet (see appendix C-3 in volume II) has a row for recording the depth of the forest floor (all surface organic horizons combined). Forest floor depth can be used to determine loss of nutrients from the organic layers. If the organic layers are piled and burned, nutrients are lost from the site. Page-Dumroese et al. (2000) describe how to use the NRCS soil data to determine approximate nutrient amounts and potential losses. Depending on site variability, you can collect this value for some (e.g., every 10 points) or all of the points. Measure the forest floor depth with a pocket ruler.

Displacement

Forest Floor

Record if the forest floor is impacted (e.g., if the surface organic matter has been moved from one place to another) on the *Data*

Entry worksheet (see appendix C-3 in volume II). The item reads "forest floor impacted." Record either a "0" (forest floor is not impacted) or a "1" (forest floor is impacted) in this row for each monitoring point. Large areas of displaced forest floor can lead to changes in nutrient cycling or erosion. Changes in the distribution and depth of the forest floor will change the soil disturbance severity rating. If the area of forest floor displacement is large, measure the area (length times average width) and enter the result into the ONSITE portion of the database to determine areal extent.

Mineral Soil

Record removal of the top mineral soil under "topsoil displacement." Record either a "0" (displacement is absent) or a "1" (displacement is present) in this row for each monitoring point. Mineral top soil displacement and gouging can result in degradation of site quality by exposing unfavorable subsoil material (e.g., denser, lower in nutrients, less organic matter, calcareous), altering slope hydrology, and causing excessive erosion and, therefore, a loss of nutrients. Displacement that has removed most of the surface soil and exposed the subsoil is considered severity class 3. The impacts of mineral soil displacement on long-term productivity are governed by slope gradient, slope complexity, and subsoil conditions.

Changes in the soil disturbance categories are based on mixing of topsoil with the subsoil, topsoil removal, and evidence of gouging and piling. This attribute is the only one specifically linked to an areal extent in most regional soil quality standards and guidelines. Document the areal extent used by individuals before monitoring and list it in the comment field. Because the electronic field form is used to calculate ongoing sample size using "0s" and "1s," areal extent size must be listed elsewhere. For example, if the regional soil quality standards lists an areal extent (e.g., >1.5 m (5 ft) in diameter), then use that areal extent for counting mineral soil displacement (counted as "1" [present] on the worksheet). In addition, if areas of mineral soil displacement are extraordinarily large, measure them for area (length multiplied by the average width) and enter the result into the ONSITE calculator.

Point Attributes

After recording information about forest floor impacted, use the section on the *Data Entry* worksheet (see appendix C-3 in volume II) that asks for information about live plants, invasive species, fine woody material, coarse woody material, bare soil, and rock. These attributes are meant to help describe site conditions that may indicate a change in site sustainability or erosion potential. These attributes are not automatically included in the sample size calculation on the *Variable Selection* worksheet (see appendix C-2). If these attributes are important for particular sites, however, they may be included in the sample size calculation.

Erosion

Record erosion in the *Data Entry* worksheet (see appendix C-3 in volume II) under "erosion." Record either a "0" (absent) or a "1" (present) in this row for each monitoring point. Soil erosion is the movement of soil by water and wind. Accelerated erosion (erosion caused by human activity that is more than the historic erosion rate) causes both onsite (soil loss, nutrient loss, lower productivity, shallower mineral soil) and offsite (reduced stream water quality, increased sedimentation, loss of aquatic habitat) impacts.

Erosion noted in the FSDMP is for surface soils within an activity area. It is not designed for roads, ditches, or places where the subsoil is exposed. The degree and extent (slight, moderate, or severe) of erosion will place this attribute into different soil disturbance (severity) categories.

Prescribed Fire and Pile Burning

Record fire severity on the *Data Entry* worksheet (see appendix C-3 in volume II) in the three rows that list fire severity (light, moderate, and severe). Determine the fire severity of the monitoring point and record a "1" (present) in the cell for that point. Record a "0" in each of the other two rows.

Broadcast Burning

Broadcast burns across the activity area will likely create a mosaic of site conditions. Low-severity burns will likely not alter soil processes for an extensive period of time. Hotter burns may impact both the forest floor and mineral soil material. As burn severity increases, the soil disturbance class (1, 2, or 3) also increases.

Pile Burning

Piles of waste logging materials, brush, or tree tops (slash) that remain after harvest activities are often burned in the activity area or on landings and skid trails. It may be difficult to describe conditions under the burned area if substantial slash remains, but it is critical to assess the size (width multiplied by the length or diameter) of the area. Use ONSITE to help calculate the size of these features. Because monitoring points may land on different piles, assess them independently for severity. Assess burn piles similarly to broadcast burning severity.

Although wildfires are not considered as part of the FSDMP, record the impacts of fire on the soil resource during preactivity assessments to help determine if mitigation measures may be necessary.

Assigning a Disturbance Class

Soil disturbance classes are assigned using visual surface characteristics and they are recorded for each monitoring point in the survey. The disturbance classes are defined in the previous sections and table 2. Table 3 also provides a list of the visual attributes of each soil indicator and some potential management-induced changes. Data collected at each monitoring point provide a representative sample of the activity area. The percentage of the activity area in each soil disturbance class is automatically calculated in the electronic worksheets and the results are displayed on the *Results* worksheet (see appendix C-4 in volume II). Reliability is estimated from the variance among estimated point proportions of each condition class. At some points, there may be a variety of soil disturbances. The observer must evaluate these overlapping indicators so that the soil disturbance class best represents the point.

Literature Cited

Fleming, R.L.; Powers, R.F.; Foster, N.W. et al. 2006. Effects of organic matter removal, soil compaction, and vegetation control on 5-year seedling performance: a regional comparison of Long-Term Soil Productivity sites. Canadian Journal of Forest Research. 36: 5429–5450.

Gomez, A.; Powers, R.F.; Singer, M.J. et al. 2002 Soil compaction effects on growth of young ponderosa pine following litter removal in California's Sierra Nevada. Soil Science Society of America Journal. 66: 1334–1343.

McNab, W.H.; Cleland, D.T.; Freeouf, J.A. et al., comps. 2007. Description of ecological subregions: sections of the conterminous United States [CD-ROM]. Gen. Tech. Rep. WO-76B. Washington, DC: U.S. Department of Agriculture, Forest Service. 80 p.

Napper, C.; Howes, S.; Page-Dumroese, D. et al. [N.d.]. Soil disturbance field guide. Manuscript in preparation. 0820 1815-SDTDC. San Dimas, CA: San Dimas Technology Center.

Page-Dumroese, D.; Jurgensen, M.; Elliot, W. et al. 2000. Soil quality standards and guidelines for forest sustainability in northwestern North America. Forest Ecology and Management. 138: 445–462.

Page-Dumroese, D.S.; Jurgensen, M.F.; Tiarks, A.E. et al. 2006. Soil physical property changes at North American Long-Term Soil Productivity study sites: 1 and 5 years after compaction. Canadian Journal of Forest Research. 36: 551–564.

Powers, R.F.; Tiarks, A.E.; Boyle, J.R. 1998. Assessing soil quality: practical standards for sustainable forest productivity in the United States. In: Adams, M.B.; Ramakrishna, K.; Davidson, E., eds. The contribution of soil science to the development and implementation of criteria and indicators of sustainable forest management. SSSA Spec. Publ. 53. Madison, WI: Soil Science Society of America: 53–80.

U.S. Department of Agriculture, Natural Resources Conservation Service (USDA NRCS). 1993. Soil survey manual. Rev. Agricultural handbook 18. Washington, DC: U.S. Department of Agriculture, Natural Resources Conservation Service, Soil Survey Staff. 437 p.

Appendix A. Safety of Hazard Analysis

1. WORK PROJECT/ ACTIVITY Soil Quality Monitoring	2. LOCATION
4. NAME OF ANALYST	5. JOB TITLE

8. HAZARDS	9. ABATEMENT ACTIONS Engineering Controls • Substitution • Administrative Controls • PPE
Communication breakdown	Never travel or work alone in isolated areas without preparing and discussing a detailed JHA that includes emergency evacuation procedures and a communication plan. Talk to each other. Let other crew members know when you see a hazard. Avoid working near known hazard trees. Yell "ROCK!" if you see one start to roll down the hill. Always know the whereabouts of fellow crew members. Review emergency evacuation procedures (see below). Carry a radio and spare batteries. Ensure that local frequencies and repeaters are programmed in radios. Contact local districts or resource areas prior to field work to determine appropriate communication protocols. If going to a remote area alone, let someone know specifically where you will be; be sure someone knows you have returned.
Overdue, no contact, missing	File itinerary of planned routes of travel, destination, ETD/ETA, employee names, emergency phone numbers/communication system and contact points, and checkin/checkout system.
Falling down, twisted ankles and knees, poor footing, and general slips, trips, and falls	Always watch your footing. Slow down and use extra caution around logs, rocks, and animal holes. Steep slopes (>20%) can be hazardous under wet or dry conditions. Wear laced boots with nonskid, Vibram®-type soles for ankle support and traction. Stretch before hiking.

Crossing creeks, seeps, bogs, wet logs, wet rocks, wet vegetation slopes, and wet ash slopes	Watch where you walk in streams, expect rocks to be slippery, and do not cross if you feel unsafe. Cross facing upstream so knees do not buckle; use a stick for extra balance. Expect mud and vegetation-covered water to be deeper than it appears. Expect logs to be slippery, especially when the bark is worn off. Expect trails in wet areas to give way to pressure near toe slopes. Keep limber and alert at all times. Be aware in areas of wet ash, loose rocks, and unstable slopes. Slopes with wet vegetation are frequently slick and hazardous.
Stobs, sharp limbs, and other puncturing objects	Long pants, good boots, and cautious attention will mitigate the danger of possible punctures and tears associated from stobs. Puncture wounds are particularly difficult to clean completely in the field; monitor closely for swelling and throbbing. Obtain medical treatment if these conditions persist. Always expect hidden stobs in dense vegetation. Learn to roll; do not use arms to break a fall. As an option, cutting pant legs may reduce falls associated with stobs.
Falling objects	When applicable, wear a hardhat for protection from falling limbs and pinecones and from tools and equipment carried by other crew members. Always wear a hardhat in burned areas, high snag density areas, falling rock areas, and high wind situations. Try to stay out of the woods during extremely high winds.
Damage to eyes	Watch where you walk, especially around trees and brush with limbs sticking out. Exercise caution when clearing limbs from tree trunks. Wear eye protection.
Bee and wasp stings	Watch for respiratory problems. Notify dispatcher/ other crew members/supervisor and get person to a doctor immediately if he/she has trouble breathing. Always know where the first aid kit is. Gently scrape stinger off if one is present. Apply analgesic swab and cold pack, if possible, and watch for infection. Flag the location of any known nests and inform other crew members. Carry antihistamine and asthma inhaler for bee stings. If known allergy, carry proper medication and instruct co-workers in administration.

Ticks and infected mosquitoes	Wear long-sleeved shirts. Tuck pants into socks/boots.
	Visually check each other for ticks while in the field. Check yourself carefully at home at day's end. Use repellent at your discretion.
	If a tick is imbedded in you:
	• Gently pull the tick out with tweezers or fingernails, using a quick tug.
	• Ensure tick head is removed.
	• Wash the infected area and monitor for a red rash.
	• Monitor the tick bite for inflammation, color alteration, or swelling.
	See a doctor if problems present themselves.
Heat stress	Remain constantly aware of the four basic factors that determine the degree of heat stress (air temperature, humidity, air movement, and heat radiation) relative to the surrounding work environmental heat load.
	Drink enough water or sports drinks to keep hydrated and prevent heat exhaustion or heat stroke (at least 2 quarts in summer). Consumption of caffeine and alcohol greatly increase susceptibility to dehydration. Limit these intakes before and during exposure to heat stress.
	Know the signs and symptoms of heat exhaustion, heat cramps, and heat stroke. Heat stroke is a true medical emergency requiring immediate emergency response action.
	NOTE: The severity of the effects of a given environmental heat stress is decreased by reducing the work load, increasing the frequency and/or duration of rest periods, and introducing measures that will protect employees from hot environments.
Cold extremes	Cover all exposed skin and be aware of frostbite. Although cold air will not freeze the tissues of the lungs, slow down and use a mask or scarf to minimize the effect of cold air on air passages.
	Additional measures to take to avoid cold weather problems—
	a. Dress in layers with wicking garments (those that carry moisture away from the body) and a weatherproof slicker. A wool or breathable synthetic outer garment is recommended.

	b. Take layers off as you heat up; put them on as you cool down.
	c. Wear head protection that provides adequate insulation and protects the ears.
	d. Maintain your energy level. Avoid exhaustion and overexertion, which causes sweating, dampens clothing, and accelerates loss of body heat and increases the potential for hypothermia (the lowering of the body's core temperature).
	e. Acclimate to the cold climate to minimize discomfort.
	f. Maintain adequate water/fluid intake to avoid dehydration.
Wind	Windchill greatly affects heat lose. Avoid working in old, decomposed timber, especially hardwoods, during periods of high winds due to snag hazards. Wind also exacerbates the likelihood of hypothermia. Always carry appropriate rain gear (both jacket and pants), because rain gear greatly mitigates the effects of windchill.
Rain	Always carry appropriate rain gear (both jacket and pants). Hypothermia is much more likely when moisture is directly on or near the skin.
Sun rays	Ultraviolet light from the sun can be damaging to the eyes; look for sunglasses that specify significant protection from UV-A and UV-B radiation.
	Ultraviolet light from the sun can be damaging to the skin and lead to sunburn or skin cancer; on bright, sunny days and overcast days, always carry and apply to exposed skin, SPF 15-rated sun block lotion, a wide-brimmed hat, long-sleeved shirt, and pants to mitigate harmful light rays on the skin.
Lightning	Check weather report; stay off ridge tops and open slopes during lightning storms. If stuck in open, keep radio and metallic objects away from you, squat down with only feet on ground using insulating pad if possible, and keep as much of your body off the ground as possible. Never use radios or cell phones in lightning. Stay away from large trees that may act as lighting rods. Look for cover in even-aged tree stands. Above all else, stay out of streams during lighting activity, and do not carry stadia rods or other survey tools—graphite, fiberglass, aluminum, and wood can all attract lighting, especially when wet. Never use any electronic devices during lightning activity.

Environmental hazards	Choose campsites that are free of snags and leaning green trees and that have no danger of rolling rocks, slides, and flash floods.
Animal problems	Do not camp in areas with known animal problems. Hang food and follow food and cooking guidelines when in bear country. Keep a clean camp, do not leave food out, and clean up spills.
Ecological impacts	Follow "leave no trace" guidelines to minimize impacts from camping.
Giardia cryptosporidium and other parasites	Drink filtered or tap water at all times. Boil water if you do not have a filter or access to clear potable tap water, or use iodine tablets.
Fatigue, carelessness	Get plenty of sleep at night. Be careful and do the job right the first time, safely.
Wounds, scrapes, bruises, sprains, rashes, burns, infections, and general ailments	Carefully clean all cuts, punctures, scrapes, and such with antiseptic. Dress with clean bandages, replacing as necessary. Closely monitor all wounds, taking caution not to worsen them by continued physical activity. If ill, do not continue exertion and worsen the ailment. Take special care not to pass contagious ailments to fellow workers. Notify other crew members and immediate supervisor of all accidents, illnesses, and wounds, including those obtained before going on a tour. If applicable, this notification should take place before departing into the backcountry.
Toilet paper and feminine hygiene waste materials	These items, when used or unused, and if scented, must be considered attractants for animals, but carry the added weight of being considered biohazardous waste when used. Handle disposal of these items in one of two ways: (1) pack it in, pack it out—dedicate two plastic zipping or Ziploc® bags for this method or (2) dig a 4-in by 6-in cat hole to bury items along with waste.
Blisters and other foot injuries	These wounds are quite common in the back-country and should be planned for. Plenty of clean, dry socks should be on hand (two for each day if you are prone to blisters). Regular changing of socks prevents blisters and reduces infection of existing ones. In addition, thick moisture-wicking socks with thin, nylon liners are quite useful for preventing blisters. Break in boots before the start of the field season as well. Proper-fitting boots are essential. Always carry moleskin, rubbing alcohol, and duct tape for mitigating these problems.

Trash	The survey crew will pack out all trash. Treat all food-oriented trash the same as food in terms of wildlife attraction.
Other trash, left by other people	It is encouraged to pick up other trash found during surveys, but exercise extreme caution when doing so. Broken glass and the edges of tin cans can be hazardous. There are reports of bottles fermenting in the sun and building pressure, only to shatter and send glass fragments flying when disturbed by trash collection. Thus, gloves, eye protection, and long-sleeved shirt and pants are good ideas when handling trash.
Methamphetamine remains	It has come to the attention of law enforcement that many illegal drug producers are using national forests as ground upon which to make illegal drugs. Specifically, methamphetamine, also known as crystal meth, remains or trash have been found on a much more frequent basis. Thus, any trash that may appear suspicious or that emits toxic odors should be avoided and located on the map. A report to the local LEO is in order for such suspicious trash. The Forest Service course on recognizing and dealing with methamphetamine hazards is recommended.
Marijuana	Forest Service employees are advised, when encountering marijuana growing on national forest property, to leave the vicinity carefully, cautiously, and immediately. In some cases, these areas have been known to be guarded and/or booby-trapped. Notify local LEO immediately.
Communication	For cases in which evacuation is needed, communication procedures are essential. Know how to use the radio and who to contact in an emergency.
Medical evacuation	For cases in which injury, illness, or accident initiates the need to evacuate a person, the first priority is to contact other crews in the area for assistance, and then contact emergency crews from the district office or supervisor's office. If the wounded person is mobile, the crew should calmly and steadily proceed by the most direct and easy route to the vehicles in an effort to get to professional medical care. If the hurt crew member is not mobile, make preparations for backcountry extraction by a search and rescue team. In either case, if there is no radio contact, a crew member should be dedicated to hiking to the ridge to get

	a radio signal out. If search and rescue must intervene, be prepared with GPS coordinates and legal description of the location. Also plan to send a healthy crew member to the vehicles to assist search and rescue in locating the wounded crew member. Always remember your backcountry safety training during these times, and remember to think cool, calm, and collected. The atmosphere of the accident often instills shock, so mitigate shock by providing a relaxed, attentive, and well-thought-out atmosphere.
Danger evacuation	If weather, wildlife, human, or other dangers cause a need for evacuation, the group should stay together and proceed to safe quarters. Use your safety briefings about shelter areas and communication in case of these events; you will be trained for such occasion.
Once to the vehicle	Look at additional evacuation measures regarding vehicle safety, but always remember that driving should be cautious, even in the face of an accident or dangerous situation.
10. LINE OFFICER SIGNATURE	11. TITLE

ETA = estimated time of arrival. ETD = estimated time of departure. GPS = Global Positioning System. JHA = job hazard analysis. LEO = law enforcement organization. SPF = sun protection factor.